MARY'S FUNNY REAL ESTATE STORIES

MARY MAXIE

MARY'S FUNNY REAL ESTATE STORIES

Mary is a realtor in Phoenix Arizona, although she also sold real estate in Calgary, Alberta, Canada. Through the years, Mary has collected stories that:

Make you laugh!

Make you say 'E-w-w-w'!

Make you say "Oh my God!"

Make you say "Are you kidding me?"

Make you think "And these people walk the earth, vote, reproduce and participate in real estate transactions!?!!"

She has been blogging and facebooking these stories for years, and people have been asking her to compile them into a book, so here you go! If you have ever been a realtor, inspector, escrow officer, lawyer, house builder, or bought or sold a house, you'll identify with at least a few of these house stories. And they are all true, believe it or not!

ABOUT THE E-BOOK YOU HAVE PURCHASED:

Your non-refundable purchase of this e-book allows you to only ONE LEGAL copy for your own personal reading on your own personal computer or device. **You do not have resell or distribution rights without the prior written permission of both the publisher and the copyright owner of this book.** This book cannot be copied in any format, sold, or otherwise transferred from your computer to another through upload to a file sharing peer to peer program, for free or for a fee, or as a prize in any contest. Such action is illegal and in violation of the U.S. Copyright Law. Distribution of this e-book, in whole or in part, online, offline, in print or in any way or any other method currently known or yet to be invented, is forbidden. If you do not want this book anymore, you must delete it from your computer.

WARNING: The unauthorized reproduction or distribution of this copyrighted work is illegal. Criminal copyright infringement, including infringement without monetary gain, is investigated by the FBI and is punishable by up to 5 years in federal prison and a fine of $250,000.

If you find a Durragraphics e-book being sold or shared illegally, please let us know at mary@marymaxie.com

A Durragraphix Inc book

Copyright © 2014 by Mary Maxie
Print ISBN:
First E-book Publication: July 2014
Cover design by Laurena Kiesz

ALL RIGHTS RESERVED: This literary work may not be reproduced or transmitted in any form or by any means, including electronic or photographic reproduction, in whole or in part, without express written permission. All characters and events in this book are fictitious. Any resemblance to actual persons living or dead is strictly coincidental.

PUBLISHER

Durragraphix Inc
PO Box 1146
Phoenix, AZ 85022

Letter to Readers

Dear Readers,

If you have purchased this copy of *Mary's Funny Real Estate Stories* by Mary Maxie, thank you for not sharing your copy of this book.

Regarding E-book Piracy

This book is copyrighted intellectual property. No other individual or group has resale rights, auction rights, membership rights, sharing rights, or any kind of rights to sell or to give away a copy of this book.

The author and the publisher work very hard to bring our paying readers high-quality reading entertainment. This is Mary Maxie's livelihood. It's fair and simple. Please respect Ms.Maxie's right to earn a living from her work.

MARY'S FUNNY REAL ESTATE STORIES

Chapter 1 Strange Buyer Experiences

Chapter 2 Strange Seller Experiences

Chapter 3 Naked, Yes, Buck Naked

Chapter 4 Hoarders and Collectors

Chapter 5 Pet Lovers

Chapter 6 A Funny Thing Happened While I Was Out Showing Houses…

Chapter 7 A Funny Thing Happened at my Open House…

Chapter 8 People Make You Crazy

Chapter 9 Horror Stories

Chapter 10 Snake Stories

Chapter 11 Realtor versus Nature

Chapter 12 Realtor versus Realtor

Chapter 13 Stories that Don't fit Anywhere Else But I Wanted To Include

Introduction

I have been in the real estate industry for many years. I always like to find the humor in situations, and real estate has offered up more humor than any other field I have engaged in during my checkered career. Most of the stories are mine, but occasionally other realtors send me stories as well. Most are funny, some are poignant, some are scary, but all are entertaining.

I hope you enjoy them, and I'm working on a second volume, so please send me any stories you think would be good to include. I promise I will edit for grammar and spelling, and I'll alter slightly so you won't get sued by anyone. If you wish, I'll thank you in the acknowledgements, but if you want to be anonymous, that's okay too, just be sure and note that when you send me stories at marymaxieauthor@hotmail.com

Chapter 1 Strange Buyer Experiences

Are you pulling my leg?

I was out showing houses & my clients wanted to have lunch. We stopped for lunch at a famous chain restaurant, and were seated in a booth.

My (male) client sat down & asked if I minded if he took off his leg, as it was bothering him. I was somewhat taken aback, because even though he had shorts on, his leg was so realistic I hadn't noticed that it was a prosthesis. I fumbled an affirmative reply, and was shocked when he actually removed his leg and stood it up on the seat beside him. I think the wait person was in shock and managed to tell everyone on staff that there was a leg sitting in the booth, as they all found excuses to fill our water glasses, remove plates, and ask if we wanted anything else over the course of our meal.

When we were ready to leave, my client placed his leg on the bench, and re-attached his prosthesis.

You just never know what is going to happen when you are showing houses!

It's Just Too Hot!

It's hard to explain to out of town buyers just how hot it is showing houses in the desert, especially in summer, when temperatures can reach 115 degrees, and most houses are vacant, meaning there is no water turned on, and no air conditioning.

One couple couldn't take the heat after several hours of looking at houses, and the house we were viewing was vacant, with a very inviting, clear pool out back. I thought they were just going to dangle their feet in the water to see how warm it was, but before I knew it, they had stripped down to their underwear, and jumped in! Not exactly what I expected. After cooling off, they went into the bathroom in the house, took off their wet undies, and dressed, ready for the next house. I couldn't get the thought of both of them going commando for the rest of the day, out of my mind!

Who's In First?

In a sellers' market, you have to be inventive and creative when looking for a house. One realtor told me she was taking a listing, when she got a call on her cell phone. It was another realtor, sitting in her car, outside the house, who had noticed the first realtor's car in the driveway, had seen the magnetic sign on the car door, and had called the number. The first words out of her mouth were, "Did you get the listing signed yet? If so, my clients and I are in the driveway and we want to look at the house." The sellers agreed, and the house was sold within about fifteen minutes of when the listing was signed!

Hurricanes in Arizona?

That's what it felt like for one showing. It was during a high sellers' market, and houses were going as fast as they were listed. My client had missed out on several houses because we couldn't get there to look at them in time, and they already had several offers by the time we viewed the houses.

I spotted the perfect house for him about 9 pm and figured it would be gone by the time he was finished work the next day. I called him & said I'd meet him there now, in the dark, with gale force winds blowing. I took a couple of big flashlights, and we both stumbled around in the dark trying to find the lockbox, which was cleverly hidden behind some large prickly bushes.

We got in, looked at the house by flashlight, wrote an offer by flashlight, called the listing realtor who only lived two doors down. I took the offer to her, she called her seller, and we had the offer accepted then and there. She told me later that had we waited till morning or some time the next day, there were seven or eight offers and we would have lost out again.

Through a Glass Darkly

Strangely enough we don't have to show houses at night very often in Arizona. However, in Alberta, where days are very short in the winter, we often showed houses at night. Before the days of electronic offers, and back when we used to present offers to the sellers in person, I remember many times signing offers on the hood of cars, and presenting them to the seller, then going back outside to sign a counter offer, also on the hood of the car, and back and forth till all parties agreed.

Sometimes it works well for the seller and buyer to meet...

My clients and I arrived to view their perfect house, at the same moment as the seller's realtor arrived to present an offer from another party. The seller refused to look at the offer until my clients had a look at the house. The seller and my buyer loved each other, and were happily discussing where was the best location for the Christmas tree in December, while the seller's realtor fumed about not getting to present the other offer. The seller then announced that she wouldn't look at the other offer, as she loved my clients, and as long as the price we were offering was in the ball park, she wanted my people to have it.

...And sometimes it's a disaster.

Buyer and seller lived in the same neighborhood, and had a nodding acquaintance. However, once negotiations began, the situation deteriorated quickly. The buyers would walk their baby and dog past 'their' new house, and if my seller was outside watering flowers or mowing grass, shouting matches ensued! The buyers' realtor and I tried to keep them apart, but nastiness escalated until I was sure one of them would strangle the other! We finally got both our brokers and a couple of lawyers involved to settle the sale, although not without a lot of yelling, threats, and unpleasantness all around. I still believe that was the worst sale I ever had! There are at least four other stories in this book about these two parties, but I'll leave you to see if you can figure out which ones they are.

Then again, sometimes it works!

When the buyers arrived, there were at least six other realtors with buyers circling the house like vultures, waiting to get in and view it. This was also during a time when sellers could just about name any price or condition. It happened that these buyers actually knew the seller too. The wife put in a call to the seller, telling him they were bringing an offer that was $10,000 over list price, and asked if he would wait to see them before making a decision.

He agreed, and all parties met the next morning at the seller's office. He tossed aside five other offers, some higher than ours, and accepted ours, because he knew my people and wanted them to have it.

Chapter 2 Strange Seller Experiences

Hush Little Baby, Don't You Cry

My buyers were looking at a house they loved, but we were puzzled by a bronze plaque on the kitchen floor. On closer examination, we saw that the seller's baby had been born on that spot. Apparently the ambulance didn't get there in time! In the extra information offered in the contract, we asked them to please make sure and take the plaque with them and repair the holes in the kitchen floor.

#####

Apparently having babies at home is not that uncommon. I sold another house where the seller was a midwife and natural birth proponent. She had a separate room set up for birthing, and several babies, including her own, were born there. Most people wouldn't mind that, but some buyers found it weird, and the sellers told me several buyers had backed out when they found out about the births in these two houses.

Personally I'd rather live in a house where people were born instead of died. I don't always agree with clients, but I always respect their wishes.

Follow the Yellow Brick Road?

It took my buyers and me a while to figure out why a house we were looking at, had gray carpet throughout, but there were paths of tile like a yellow brick road through all the rooms. It seems that the previous owner was wheelchair bound, and only used the pathways to get around.

I would think that it would have been cheaper to tile the whole house instead of just the pathways, but maybe they thought they were saving money by only tiling the traffic areas.

Clothes and Shoes, Shoes and Clothes...

My two female buyers, mother and daughter, pulled up to the house. The seller was just leaving, and took great pains to tell us that she was using the second bedroom as a walk in closet, but that it could easily be turned back into a bedroom.

But what a walk in closet! On three walls there were built in commercial shoe shelves from floor to ceiling. The shoes were arranged according to color, and within each color grouping, they were arranged by purpose (walking, dancing, fashion, winter, summer, boots, sports, etc.). We stopped counting at 300 pairs of ladies shoes in every color of the rainbow. (And I thought I was Imelda). The actual closet in the room had its door removed and commercial racks for displaying bags and purses were attached to the wall. We didn't count the purses, but they included cross-body, hobo, sports, totes, clutches, satchels, evening, shoulder bags, leather, cloth, straw, silk, canvas and anything else you could imagine, all in colors corresponding to the shoes.

In the center of the room were round commercial racks for clothing, all in the same size. My clients who were more familiar with high end jeans than I am, announced that there were 29 pairs of $700./pair jeans hanging there. I wonder how many pairs you can wear at a time! Or even in the course of a month!

The other closets in the home were equally full of clothes. One closet was all formal wear, one had all sports and gym wear, and another had all coats, including several furs.

And lest you think there might have been more than one person living there, not so. Just one shopaholic!

Pigeons Take Over Mansion

Wow! What a steal! MLS stated $400,000 house needed finishing, which was an understatement to say the least. The previous owner had torn down 3 houses to build this dream mansion, but according to internet stories & the neighbors, he had been sent to jail for mortgage fraud a couple of years ago, leaving his dream home unfinished.

The most impressive thing about the house was the size– close to 10,000 sq ft, and the double front doors, which were 16 feet high, heavy black & gold metal & glass, with a two foot medallion/knocker in the center of each. A neighbor told us the doors (3 in all) cost $20,000. apiece. However, the house had been abandoned at framing stage, & had been open to the elements & critters for years. There was pigeon poop everywhere (and I mean everywhere) along with a few dead birds here and there, so a disgusting smell pervaded every corner of the house, despite being open to the elements.

You could see the design and architecture were exquisite & the house would have been a showplace if it had ever been finished off. We figured the house would need at least another million to finish, but after being open to elements for a couple of years, would likely have to be demolished, so no sale. It was also tied up with banks, mortgage companies, lawyers, the courts, bankruptcy proceedings and more, so another reason not to buy it.

Sellers leave behind the strangest things

We were touring an empty house, and only a buyer as tall as my client would have seen this on the top shelf of the kitchen cupboard. It was a huge, though very dull, samurai sword, apparently forgotten by the movers. We left it there and notified the listing agent to perhaps get it out of there in case someone decided to steal it or use it. I hope they didn't find any other weapons left behind!

####

One realtor told me he was previewing a house that had been recently vacated. It was a mess, with lots of garbage all over. There was something long and shiny lying along the wall in the hallway. He thought it was just more debris, but it turned out to be the owners' pet snake, asleep, that they had left behind. The reason he didn't recognize it right away as a snake, was that it wasn't coiled, but lying flat and straight right up against the baseboard.

#####

In another empty house, an apparently unused closet had a fully stocked bar in it, with several hundred dollars worth of liquor for the taking. We considered having a party, but in the end, just notified the lister to come get it all.

Check Your Weapons At the Door...

A guy needs a carpet restorer, because he's moving out next week, and his shotgun which was stored under the bed, accidentally went off, damaging the carpet! He's lucky that's all it damaged!

More Gun Stories...

Realtor arrived with clients to show a supposedly empty house. They were greeted at the door by a rifle and handgun toting female who rudely asked what they wanted. The seller had moved out, and kindly offered the house to his neighbors, who were flooded out of their own house, but didn't tell the neighbors that people might come by to look at the house while they were in residence. The buyers decided they didn't want to have neighbors who had guns and weren't shy about using them, so that house got a pass.

####

A home inspector was going about his business, climbing on the roof, looking at the open garage, when the local police arrived, guns in hand, and demanded that he put up his hands. It seems a neighbor had alerted the boys in blue that there was a strange man in the house. The inspector was finally

allowed to go to the truck and show them his work order and his super key, so they were satisfied, but he was still plenty rattled.

Fire In The Hole!

There was a house in Phoenix where a former serviceman lived. He decided to dig a foxhole in the back yard, but it soon morphed into so much more. It became a man cave (literally), as he dug side tunnels, created a retractable roof over the ten foot diameter hole, added a ladder, furniture, electricity by way of several long extension cords to power his floor lamps, a small fridge, hotplate, TV, plus running water by way of a garden hose, etc. He had a latrine with chemical toilet, and a bed. One has to wonder if he ever left his little cave, but I guess he needed food and beer once in a while.

Anyhow, when he died, the whole cave came to light & created quite a stir, but I never did hear if the bank that took over the house had to fill in the hole, or if some other buyer wanted it left as is!

If It's Not Nailed Down...

The rules when selling a house state that all permanent fixtures have to stay when the seller leaves. That means curtain rods, door knobs, really anything that is actually attached to the house or yard. Usually that includes plants planted in the yard as well.

However, the word 'attached' has different meanings to different people and different lawyers. One buyer complained to a lawyer that the seller had removed all the large flower pots in the yard. Flower pots are not usually attached, so are considered personal property and therefore removable. This buyer's lawyer argued that the pots had drip watering systems attached to each pot, and that therefore, the pots were attached. You decide how you would solve this dispute!

#####

Another realtor told me this story. Back in the day, the height of luxury in the kitchen was a built in blender. They also had toasters and can openers that you could access by a flat cover in the countertop that allowed the appliances to rise up to counter level. Some of them pulled out of the walls. They lost popularity quickly, because of the difficulty in repairing and servicing them. If you couldn't get parts, you had to destroy the whole counter or wall to take them out.

In any case, this realtor represented the seller, who had one of these built in blenders. She was selling the house, but didn't want to sell her blender. She had

been hoarding extra parts for it, and wanted to take it with her, refusing to fix the resulting hole in the counter. It was firmly attached, so the buyer thought it should belong to her. The blender fight threatened to derail the whole deal, until the seller's husband (quietly and under the table) handed over the cash to fix the damage, telling the realtor not to tell his wife about it!

Our State Tree and Flower

I arrived to show a house and couldn't see the house for Sahuaro cacti, on all sides. The owner was pretty prickly about showing his house and forest too. And you can't get rid of them because they are AZ's state tree/flower. I guess you'd have to find a buyer who liked the cacti forest as well as the present owner.

Chapter 3 Naked, Yes, Buck Naked!

No Shirt, No Shoes, No Pants, No Sale!

I showed a house where there was a naked 500 (at least) pound man watching TV in the living room. He may have had undershorts on, but there was nothing visible that we could see around the fat rolls. He knew ahead of time we were coming to see the house, and it would have been nice if he had put a shirt on. My buyers were completely turned off that he didn't seem to care what we thought. He didn't even turn the TV down. I usually set up a signal phrase with buyers to tell me when they just want to get out of the house quickly without looking any further. We use the phrase when there are sellers present in the house and we don't want them to know our code phrase. We didn't stay long at that one.

Beach Bunnies Ahoy!

I had made an appointment with the sellers, and when we got there to look at the house, I knocked, called out, and entered with my clients. We spotted, through the family room window, two good looking young females swimming naked in the pool. I went outside to tell them we were in the house. They were sure embarrassed, and scrambled to get their swim suits on. The mother of one of them was the seller, and hadn't bothered to let her daughter know there would be people there to view the house.

Splish Splash, I Was Taking a Bath...

I rang, opened the door, and called out, in case someone was home, and a woman who had been showering came out to greet us with just a towel around herself. I did phone ahead, so why was she so surprised to see us? And not the least bit embarrassed! Just asked us to look at the master bedroom last, so she could get dressed.

Afternoon Delight?

There have always been rumors that realtors meet in empty houses when they are having affairs. There were no cars visible out front of this one listing, but maybe we should have been on alert since there was no key or key container in the lockbox. However, the door appeared to be ajar, so my clients and I went in and called out. We heard strange noises and muffled voices coming from the master bedroom, and so I called out again. A very upset, disheveled, surprised and embarrassed couple came out of the bedroom, handed me the lockbox key, and ran out the door to the garage, where they had parked their cars. I guess the lure of an unoccupied house, where a couple can have an anonymous rendevous, is worth more than a reprimand from the Ethics Committee we are all responsible to. They even left a half bottle of wine, two plastic wine glasses, and a box of condoms.

I called the listing realtor to give her the good news that she had to come and clean up after her unauthorized visitors. This was before the days of electronic lockboxes that allow the lister to see who has been in the house by the lockbox activity, so I doubt these two were ever caught.

More Afternoon Delight!

I think there must be more than a few sexual exhibitionists in the world. The owners knew I was bringing buyers to view the house, so must have wanted us to see them. They were in bed, TV on, middle of the day, and naked, as far as my clients and I could see. We asked if we could wait outside so they could leave, and they said it was quite all right if we toured the house, and they would stay where they were, watching TV.

We were so disconcerted that we just left, without seeing the home. I did call the lister to suggest that his sellers might want to be absent when the house was being shown.

Do Ya Think I'm Sexy?

My clients and I knocked on the door, and heard footsteps approaching, so I didn't use the lockbox key. The inner door opened, and a totally naked man answered. We told him we'd be back later, but my clients didn't want to go back after that. And he actually seemed proud of his physique, posing for us as he talked to us. My client was a female, so maybe if one of us had been male, he wouldn't have been such a poser!

X-Rated Video

A New Jersey realtor was caught on the seller's video camera feed having a sexual affair with a fellow realtor in the master bedroom This affair was recently shown on an ABC special on realtors who abuse their clients' trust. The lister's affair was filmed over a period of a couple of months, & he is now being sued by the seller. That case is still before the courts at this writing, so I haven't heard what happened in the end.

In the same piece, there were cases cited of realtors stealing jewelry and prescription drugs, plus one shown on camera rifling through the female owner's lingerie and stealing panties. There is nothing specifically in the Realtor Code of Ethics that addresses this type of thing, but it's definitely an abuse of trust.

Chapter 4 Hoarders and Collectors

But My Collection Is (Choose one) different, more interesting, more expensive, more everything, than anyone else's collection

People collect things and think everyone wants to see them. One lady had special shelves built to house a collection of thousands of dolls. Her whole basement was dedicated to dolls, some new, some old, some cheap, some expensive, some well loved and used, others still in original boxes, that she had been collecting since she was a child. It was wondrous to look at, but when you are selling a house, you want potential buyers to look at the house itself, not the personal things belonging to the seller. We want the buyer to picture themselves and their own belongings there, not be turned off by what is already there, or distracted from looking at the attributes of the house.

How Not To Sell a House- Three (Or More) Blind Mice

I was showing a house, and the first turnoff for my clients was a large cage of mice. We couldn't imagine why anyone would want to keep common field mice, but we continued to tour the house. When we got to the master bedroom, there was a large heavy shelf above the bed, with an enormous fish tank on it. In the tank was the biggest boa constrictor I had ever seen, and for a snake-o-phobic, like me, it was at least 118 feet long. We figured out what the mice in the cage were for, and beat a hasty retreat.

#####

Another house (not the same buyers, thank heavens) had a reptile room downstairs. Snakes, tarantulas, gila monsters, lizards, etc. My clients walked out and said they would always be afraid one of the reptiles would have escaped and they would find it in the wall or coming up thru the toilet.

Get rid of pets like these before the house is shown. In 99% of cases, people don't like reptiles, and we can't just advertise for those who do, and hope they will show up to view the house.

Snakes and Snails and Puppy Dog Tails

I had a house listed that was an elderly widowed lady's dream house. It was very feminine, frilly, and had a large sewing room that had been specially designed for her seamstress business.

I found a buyer for the house, who looked like a bull in a china shop in the frilly house. He was a very large tattooed biker, who was delighted that the garage was large enough for all his bikes, but he was even more delighted with the sewing room, as he told me all about his snake and reptile collection, that would fit perfectly into that room.

I didn't have the courage to tell the elderly seller what was in store for her precious sewing room, but when I told her daughter, she said it was better that her mother believe that another sweet lady would be utilizing the lovely sewing room! She said her mother wouldn't have been able to handle the idea that there were snakes in the room!

Who Let the Really Big Dogs Out?

I was glad the big dogs were gone by the time I showed a house that had doggie footprints and slobber that were taller than I am, on the patio door. And no short jokes from the peanut gallery. The prints were taller than my 6 ft client as well.

The Client is Always Right, Or Pets Come First

My client was relocating to our city, and was ensconced in a small motel room with two very large dogs and three cats. She was anxious to find a place quickly so her beloved pets could have more space.

When I arrived to pick her up to go looking at homes, she announced that we had to take her SUV, as we had to take the pets with us to see if they liked the homes she was seeing!

Okay, I have allergies to most pets, but I bravely took an antihistamine, and prepared to spend the day coughing and wheezing. However, what I was not prepared for, was that one of the large dogs apparently gets carsick if he has to ride in the back seat, so the dog was going to sit in the front seat, while I was to ride in the back with the rest of the menagerie.

I had to emphasize my allergies and take my own car, while she followed me with the pets. Of course, at every stop, we had to leash and crate all the pets, and take them into the back yards to see if they liked the houses. We finally found a house that she and the pets could agree on, and wrote an offer. I did, however, find a previous engagement so that I had to miss the house warming, as the invitees included pet friends as well as humans.

All Aboard!

A model railroad enthusiast wanted to sell his house. He had train track shelving around the perimeter of every room about a foot from the ceiling. The trains could completely circle and interconnect with every room in the entire house, and he wanted to know if I thought he should have them running when people came to view the house. There were even holes in the walls at ceiling level for the tracks to continue unimpeded through every room.

In one room that was his command center, there were waist high platforms, containing mountains, tunnels, towns, farms, and all the accoutrements of model railroading. If we could have found another model enthusiast to sell it to, it would have been a great deal. As you can imagine, showing this house was difficult, because everyone looking at it kept adding up the cost of fixing walls, removing props, etc, which would have cost thousands of dollars.

I had suggested that perhaps it would be a good idea for him to dismantle the railroads and store everything for his next home, but he was insulted that I would suggest such a thing. I think he was secretly glad that so many people would get to see his setup during the course of open houses and showings. However, it took months to sell it, and he had to significantly lower his price several times. I believe it would have been more economical for him to remove it all and repair the damage, than to keep lowering the price.

Christmas Is Coming, and Santa Claus Is Coming To Town

Another collector had hundreds of Santa Clauses from all over the world. She was so proud of her collection which covered every surface of the shelving in every room, that she didn't even take them down after the Christmas season. Again, they were wondrous to look at but very distracting for a buyer.

Also, when you take several square feet off the measurements of every room in the house by putting up shelving, you make the house look much smaller.

I'd Like To Buy The World A Coke

Don't underestimate the power of advertising. Coca Cola has been selling Coke products for decades that don't have a drop of liquid. You can buy wallpaper, cushions, salt and pepper shakers, dishes, cutlery, artwork, figurines, and all manner of collectibles. I think it becomes an obsession, and the collector is always on the lookout for more stuff to complete the collection. One particular seller had one of everything Coke sells, in her house.

Please Pass the Salt?

Another had salt and pepper shakers from all over the world. There must have been thousands of them.

ALWAYS take down your collections/hobbies before listing your house.

Books Are My Escape...

One house had so many books, there were only small paths from room to room, with books piled to the ceilings on all four walls of every room and hallway, including bathrooms and closets, making rooms half their normal size. Books were under tables, desks, beds, everywhere. To top it off there were cats on top of every pile of books. I expected an avalanche any minute.

I belong to an organization that has a huge used book sale for charity every year. I gave the sellers information about free pickups, but they told me the books were their escape, their friends, and that they could never bear to give any of them up. They were so dusty, I'm not sure any of them had ever been read.

I Never Actually Read the Books...

I took some buyers to see an upscale condo, which was touted in the MLS as being the home of an interior designer. We were very impressed with the décor, layout, price, everything, until we got to the third bedroom. We could barely get the door open and the entire room was piled to the ceiling with beautiful leather bound, gold leafed books.

I had to ask about them because they were lovely looking books, of all different sizes, shapes, and colors. The seller told me she had never actually read any of them. She explained that she used pretty books to help decorate the houses she was hired to design, so she needed lots of them to be able to choose colors and styles to match each house.

Chapter 5 Pet Lovers

Selling a Cat House

I had a listing of a wonderful house in an expensive area of million dollar houses. Lots of people were interested in the house, but when they went out into the exquisitely landscaped back yard, they were met with (mostly feral) yowling cats, cats sitting on the fence, in the trees, walking around the yard, and hiding out in the two abandoned cars in the driveway next door. The house next door was owned by two little old ladies who loved cats, fed them, and allowed them to stay, but didn't love them enough to have them spayed or neutered. Calls to animal control didn't work. Even the neighbors' BB guns didn't work! Finally calls to the two old ladies' relatives worked, the ladies moved to assisted living, the house was cleaned up, painted, & the cats disappeared. Then I got the listing for the cat house too.

The House Warming Gift

My buyers moved in, hated the barking dog next door, so they gave themselves a house warming present of a barkless dog collar, and presented it to the neighbors. No more barking. Best housewarming gift was good night's sleep for my buyers.

What Is That Tail Sticking Out and What Kind Of Animal Does It Belong To?

Out on the patio, there was a lovely brick fireplace, built-in barbecue, and built-in fridge. Underneath that structure, there were half circle holes, about like mouse holes only quite a bit bigger. From one hole, a long reptilian tail stuck out. I was tempted to leave immediately, not really wanting to see what the tail belonged to, but my clients wanted to see what it was. After poking it a couple of times with a stick, out popped not one but two large lizard type creatures. I had no idea what they were, but apparently they were the owner's pets. I retreated into the house, leaving the clients to take a closer look at the 'pets'. Would have been nice if the listing realtor had let us know to be on the lookout for them.

How NOT to sell a house: Lullaby in Birdland

I went to do a listing presentation to a lady who raises exotic birds. There were cages from floor to ceiling on all the walls of every room in the house, obviously making all the rooms much smaller than they actually were. There were also cages outside on the patio and in the garage.

The noise from the birds was deafening, sort of like being

in the rain forest. There were feathers, dust and birdseed flying everywhere, and her fans were just causing them to float and land on every surface. There was also a good amount of bird poop and bird seed everywhere. Some of the birds were out of their cages and flying around, landing on me, my paperwork, my briefcase, etc. It was complete chaos.

I gently tried to tell her that buyers wouldn't be able to even see the house, because there were so many birds and feathers etc. around. She was hurt to think I might suggest that she move the birds to another location while the house was on the market. She was offended when I said that perhaps there were lots of people (like me) who wouldn't be thrilled to have birds squawking and flying around while they were viewing the house. I turned down the listing. Can you even imagine how difficult it would be to hold an open house there?

Don't hurt your chances of selling by being too rigid in your views of your pets or other stuff after your realtor gently asks you to change something. She is not trying to offend you, but tell you what buyers want to see when they look for a new home.

Who is The Boss Here? The Dog Or The Dog People

Another dog story--The master shower had a solid three inches of dog hair packed on the floor so solidly it looked like a carpet. Apparently that was the dog's shower. The people shower was cleaner, in the other bathroom. Three inches of dog hair-- yuck!

Chapter 6 A Funny thing Happened While I Was Out Showing Houses

The Sky Is Falling Said Chicken Little

There are some strange zoning laws here in Phoenix and area. You will often find that animals and farm livestock are present in some areas.

One day, it seemed that every house we looked at had roosters crowing in the back yard, or the adjoining yards. We even saw some healthy looking chickens walking down the road in front of the houses, looking like they owned it. My clients were not interested in being awoken at the crack of dawn every day by feathery neighbors, so we altered our search criteria to avoid the chicken areas.

Old MacDonald Had A Farm

Since the zoning laws in Phoenix allow farm animal in designated areas, and since there are many people who like to live organically as much as possible, there are many homes on the market that have menageries out back, in ordinary residential neighborhoods.

One house we toured, had goats, (for the milk), chickens, a couple of sheep, and a couple of pigs. Of course, the yard smelled like a barnyard, and although it was relatively quiet when we were there, I'm sure at times, it was pretty noisy. Another big 'no' from the buyers.

Old MacDonald and the Wild West Roundup

Zoning in Phoenix allows a farmer to keep his farmland right in the middle of the city. One farmer decided to re-zone his land for housing, and actually sold two lots out of about 24, and two houses were built. One was for sale, and my clients and I arrived to find an impressive brick fence with an equally impressive wrought iron gate around the complex. Once through the gate, we arrived at the one house that was for sale. We got out of the car, and from around the corner of the house, about a dozen cows appeared, ambling over to say hello to us. My female buyer managed to literally fly into the car and lock the doors. I wasn't quite as quick, and although I am a city girl, I have a passing acquaintance with cows, so I wasn't afraid, just taken aback.

It was explained to us by the owner's realtor, that subdivided land is taxed at a much higher rate than farm land, so since he hadn't managed to sell the other lots yet, the farmer/owner could save a lot on taxes by allowing his cows to roam on the land for at least one month per year. My female buyer refused to get out of the car, so we left without looking at the house at all, since she had no wish to have cows for neighbors even for one month a year.

Niagara Falls Or Something Like It

I drove up to show a house & we saw water pouring out the garage & front doors. I called lister to get water shut off. In Phoenix, it's so hot here that mold can start growing in a day or two. It's quite dangerous, and once the mold takes hold, it's very hard to remediate, and in some severe cases, the house has to be demolished. We crossed that one off our list.

You also have to be careful to look at cracks, holes, or anything that looks like moisture might have been present at one time or another in the house. A qualified home inspector usually uses a moisture meter to ascertain whether the moisture is still present, has been repaired properly, or in some cases, if it has just been painted over. I toured one house that had black stains on the walls of the closet. I thought it might be mold, so I decided not to take my clients to see that house. It never sold, but a couple of months later, I decided to return and see if they had managed to remediate the black stuff. I looked carefully and was pretty sure they had just painted over the black, so I crossed that one off the list again.

Even a qualified inspector can't always ascertain moisture if it's well hidden. One house had mirrored tiles all over one wall. My buyers decided to renovate a few months after moving in, and when they removed the mirrored tiles, they found evidence of mold on the walls. Fortunately it was well contained, and they were able to remediate that one.

Bats In the Belfry—and That's Where They Should Stay!

My clients and I walked up to the front door of a bank-owned house that obviously no one had checked on for quite a while. There was an overhang at the front that covered the door and part of the walkway. We noticed a few black blobs on the stucco, but couldn't figure out what they might be. Bird poop? Mud? When I poked one with my pen, it moved and I jumped about six feet. It suddenly unfolded its wings to stretch about three feet! A bat! Several of them, in fact! I guess the entryway was cool and dark enough for them and we had disturbed their daily rest. The stucco provided a good foothold for them to hang onto. Needless to say, we moved on to the next house!

Dive Bombers

I usually remember to tell clients not to wear red hats outdoors in the valley, because many birds, especially hummingbirds, like the color red, and will dive bomb red hats. One time I forgot, and my client learned that the hard way. Most birds will figure out that you are not their favorite red flower before they actually hurt you, but just in case, try a different color!

Hello, Young Lovers, Wherever You Are!

All was going well at a condo showing for a couple from Canada, wanting a winter home. They were talking about how much to offer, when a rhythmic thumping was heard from the unit upstairs, especially when we were in the master bedroom, followed by lots of grunts and a few screams, ("Harder, More, Please, Oh My God…") and we realized that the floors between stories were not insulated. When the listing agent called me to get feedback on the property, I told him why my clients wouldn't be putting in an offer. He sheepishly admitted that the vocal couple upstairs was the reason his clients were selling. Disclosure issue? Maybe not legally, but morally?

Kids Do the Darnedest Things

A child of about 3 went out into the fenced back yard while parents looked over the house. A minute later, a howl was heard as the child came running toward the parents, his hands stuck together by a jumping cholla cactus. He couldn't get either hand free, and when the adults tried to unstick him, they got their own hands stuck as well. It took a while to get rid of the cactus, and at least a week for all the prickles to work their way out of his hands. They don't call them jumping cacti for nothing, as they literally seem to jump out at you!

Beware of Do-It-Yourselfers

There was a balcony over the front door of the condo. Perched precariously on the small balcony, with no railings, was a hot tub. Wht if it leaked? What if it fell down? What if someone using it, decided to get out, & fell onto the front entry below?

An overhang at the front door was being held up by a pair of crutches!

People add on rooms and other things to the house, without regard for safety. One house had a light fixture, a light switch, an outlet (presumably to plug in your electric razor?), a regular room fan, (not a shower fan), and, of all things, a motion detector all in the shower enclosure.

The seller said that the bathtub had had a leak but it was now fixed. The entire tub had been covered with duct tape!

A toilet had been added, but instead of being properly attached to the floor, it was being held in place by a bungee cord.

There was a nice looking and fairly new garage door facing out onto the driveway. However, there were stair steps leading up to the opening. Maybe you need a tank with treads to climb up into your garage?

Chapter 7 A Funny Thing Happened At My Open House

Don't Judge a Book...

I have learned not to judge books by their covers, as you can often be horribly wrong. A person walked in to my open house, and after looking around, sat down to chat with me. That's often the way, as people want to get to know the realtor a bit before opening up about their reasons for looking at the house. In this case, I was at a loss to figure out whether this person was a male or female. Long curly hair hung out from a hat, and no beard was apparent, but the huge hands were well manicured and nails polished red. The voice was either male or a female smoker with raspy voice.

Even after he/she signed the register, it wasn't apparent, as the name was also unisex. It wouldn't matter, except I usually like to address people by name or at least by Mr or Mrs, or Ms., and that wasn't possible here. He/she was charming and well-educated, and was quite happy to be called by a given name, so we had a nice conversation. Not a buyer apparently, but if it had turned into a sale, I would have been spared asking the gender, as that is something escrow asks when they need to find out how you are taking title.

Another 'Don't Judge a Book' story

A young couple dropped in to look at a house I was holding open. They were hot and sweaty after being out hiking. Any salesperson learns to 'qualify' prospects by the car they drive, jewelry, clothes, and by asking where they live now, whether they own or rent, etc. You use the clues to figure out if they can really afford the million dollar house you are sitting, of if you should try and steer them to something more in their price range. The best way to do that, of course, is to get them to talk to a lender, so you can see how much of a house they can afford.

But you learn that in a resort area such as Phoenix, people usually dress 'down', so the clues are absent. The person sitting open house with me disregarded this couple as not having any money to buy. I spoke to them and kept in touch, and they have now bought two homes from me, as well as becoming friends.

Neighbors are a source of stories about the area, and usually know everything there is to know about the people and the surroundings of the neighborhood. I have learned to always check what they say with city officials or police or whoever I need to, to get the real story. Neighbors have come to visit various of my open houses through the years and told me about divorces, domestic abuse, drug houses, murders, suicides, hoarders next door, motorcycle gangs down the street, and a hundred other things that might make selling the house difficult, or force a lower price.

On the other hand, I often find out helpful things that help sell the house faster, like how good the schools are, or how the police officer living next door will park his cruiser in the driveway when he's off duty, to discourage vandals and thieves. I have found out who the good babysitters are, which dog owner refuses to pick up his dog's refuse, which owner has the loudest dog, or the car with no muffler.

In the case of condos, neighbors will tell the realtor about coming assessments, leaky roofs, and troubles with pool vandals. And what big development is going in across the street.

All realtors will tell you about having open house signs stolen, and not always by other realtors or pranksters. Sometimes, even though state law allows open house signs, home owners and their associations will steal & destroy signs because they don't like open house traffic, or think the signs don't look dignified enough for their upscale neighborhood That kind of neighbors always talk out of the other side of their mouths when it comes time to sell their own house. Then, of course, they want as many signs as possible. On the other hand, I've had open house visitors tell me that they had stopped and propped up one of my signs that had blown over in the wind.

Chapter 8 People Make You Crazy

Bombs Away

One house had several large holes in the back yard, which looked a lot like bomb craters. No idea what they were, but why wouldn't you fill them in so people, kids and dogs wouldn't fall in, never mind people who were looking to buy the house!

Sit! Stay!

At a very nice house, the seller's well-trained dog sat in same place in hall for entire home inspection. In fact even when we wanted the dog to move so the inspector could move his ladder, the animal never moved, for the entire three hours we were there. After the inspector left, the dog must have felt the call of nature, because he finally left by way of the dog door. At that point we could see a leaking slab! Seller didn't want buyer to see it, so told the dog not to move. Thank heavens for the dog wanting to go outside, or we'd never have discovered that till after closing!

Ghost Busters

My buyer went upstairs, then came down quickly

saying it was occupied. She said there was a lady in old fashioned dress sitting in a rocker, knitting. It was empty downstairs, so I went up to see. No one there that I could see, but the rocker was still rocking. We left quickly & noticed a lady rocking in the window as we left. Honest!

Paint is Cheap!

At least that's what we always tell our clients. In this case, the sellers had painted over termite tubes throughout house, thinking we wouldn't notice vertical lines on all the walls. Only the paint was holding the house together.

Another Paint Story

Amateur painters had managed to put up blue tape on the woodwork, but then didn't take it off. Now, several years later, it's glued forever, due to time and heat-- what is the matter with people's brains?

And Another...

Hard to believe what some people do to their houses. This one probably didn't look bad when people were living there, but now that the house was empty, we could see that these lazy bones had painted around every picture, every piece of furniture, every appliance, even the toaster, so now that their stuff was gone, it was easy to see where everything used to be!

And One More...

We saw a gorgeous house in MLS. Right location, right price, all good. Got there to find that seller had issues about paint color with the Homeowners' Association, and had painted every exterior surface in hot colors of red, blue, green, purple, yellow, orange, with no two adjoining surfaces the same. Paint is cheap, but this one was a shocker as we drove up, and hard to ignore the colors to see the nice house underneath.

And Yet Another Paint Story

One couple who listed their house had allowed their teenage daughter to decorate her own room. She had spray painted the walls, ceiling, windows, and even the rug, all black! She had black bedding and curtains– it was like walking in to a cave. They had agreed to repaint the room before closing, but amazingly the buyers also had a teenage daughter who thought the room was incredibly cool! The buyers added a condition in the offer that the room was to stay 'as is'.

Poop, Poop, Everywhere

One house had so many pigeons we had to shoo them away to get in the door--feathers & poop everywhere--ugh! The house had been bank owned for a couple of years, and the bank had never done any maintenance or inspections. The birds had taken over and didn't show any signs of leaving soon. There was so much poop on the sidewalk leading in, that we were afraid we'd slip and fall, and wouldn't that be a disaster!

In another house, we could see bird poop everywhere inside the house and couldn't figure out where it came from, until we found a dead pigeon in one of the closets. I guess we found the source.

An Art Gallery, Perhaps

The house was empty, but had about 1000 picture hooks throughout. It must have been quite a gallery to see. New paint and hole filler needed immediately.

Trespassers Will Be Shot

One realtor told me about showing a house, and hearing a lot of noise from the attic. He was able to pull down the attic stairs, and climb up to see what was going on. He expected a family of squirrels or other critters, but was surprised to find the son of the former owner was entertaining his friends at a pot smoking party. What an idea! No parents to find them, no interruptions, just party, party, party!

Grow, Grow, Grow Your Crop

Parents of a teen arrived home from spending six months away for the summer, to find that their son had installed a grow-op in several seldom used closets in the house. He had taken out the drywall and replaced it with easily moveable panels, behind the closet doors, where the damage might not be noticed for some time. Inside the cavities, he planted marijuana plants and watered them and put battery operated grow lights inside. Unfortunately, the water and soil combined with the humidity created by the plants, to create mold, not to mention the parents not wanting illegal pot plants in their house. Lots of rehab needed before listing.

Dog Washing Day

We always call first when showing houses that are occupied. Nevertheless, we still find people who 'forgot' we would be looking at the house, or didn't care. You wonder if they really want to sell the house or not. We arrived to find the lady of the house washing her two very large dogs with the outdoor hose that she had brought into the house through the patio door, and copious amounts of soap suds, in the kitchen! There was water and suds everywhere, and when I asked how often she washed her pets in the house, she replied, 'All the time!' I didn't have the heart to tell her about the floor damage, and the possibility of mold inside the cupboards and in the subfloor!

If I Can't Have It, No One Can

When there were so many people being foreclosed on or having to 'short sale' their houses, there were many stories about the damage done to said houses. Lots of displaced owners figured if they couldn't have the house, they weren't going to let the bank have a nice house either. They came up with many ingenious ways to wreck the houses before they left. Even if the departing owners didn't do damage, once other opportunists figured out there was potentially valuable stuff in the house which was now abandoned, thieves went in and stripped the house, so that you never knew what you were going to find in these houses.

First, they would remove anything they could salvage, including fans, light fixtures, appliances, toilets, countertops, cabinets, sinks, taps, switch plates, register covers, copper wiring, door knobs, locks, pool equipment, hot water heaters, air conditioners, plantings, (including trees and sod) sidewalk pavers, downspouts, garage and passage doors, and even large slices of drywall, crown moldings and baseboards.

Then they would destroy anything they couldn't sell at a garage sale. One person took a chain saw and sawed horizontally through the walls, studs, doors, frames whatever, in every room, thus destroying the integrity of the whole house.

They dumped garbage in the pools, and poured oil on all the carpets.

One guy took a blowtorch to every wall and surface in the house, leaving it blackened and needing total replacement.

People poured concrete down sinks and toilets, and/or left water running after they left.

They stole pool equipment and poured concrete into the pools.

They took air conditioning units off the roof, not bothering to cover the hole left behind, and allowing debris and rain to ruin the interior.

As a sidebar to the missing air conditioning story, one buyer was told by the seller that there was a hole in the roof that needed to be repaired. Without a home inspection, she requested that the seller repair the hole, which was done. The buyer went ahead and closed on the house, and after taking possession, she couldn't figure out why the air conditioner wouldn't work. When she called an a/c person, he couldn't believe that she didn't know there was no a/c unit on the roof, just a nicely, newly repaired hole. Ask and you shall receive, but make sure you are asking for the correct repair.

Rock-A-Bye Baby

I toured a house where the king sized master bed was suspended from large hooks in the ceiling, & would rock you to sleep at night, if the ceiling didn't give way first... At least it would be easy to vacuum underneath the bed. No dust bunnies here. And maybe that would have been the solution for the couple who almost bought the condo with the noisy love making people upstairs!

If You Plant It, They Will Come?

You have to wonder whose bright idea this was. There was a triple side entry garage, with a large tree growing right in the middle of the driveway. You would have to be one great driver to miss hitting it when parking in any one of the garages. Why do people do these things?

Septic System? What Septic System?

In one house, there were two separate septic systems, both about 40-50 years old, one for the main house and the other for the guest house. It is necessary in Arizona to have the septic inspected when a house is sold, and in this case the inspector, hired by the seller, informed us that both systems were failing, that both needed to be replaced.

The seller refused to believe that the systems were inadequate, and his reasoning was "I flush the toilets and the crap disappears, so it must be working!" The inspector told him that the 'crap' was not making it to the tanks, and even so, the tanks hadn't been pumped for many years. Each new tank would have cost over $20,000, and the seller refused to be responsible for the cost. Adding to the cost was the fact that at some point, someone had decided it was a good idea to place the driveways over the tanks. So replacing the tanks would now have to include jackhammering out the driveways and then replacing the driveways, adding even more cost.

My people opted out of the deal, and I am pretty sure nothing was done about the septic problem, which is going to be a problem for the new buyer who didn't do the inspections and homework, and for the seller who didn't disclose the septic problem.

####

Another septic story: The covers for septic tanks are usually made out of some type of light weight concrete, heavy enough not to be easily dislodged by kids, but light enough to be moved if there's ever a problem with the tank. However, after many years, those covers deteriorate, becoming much more porous, until even the weight of a small child or a dog will cause them to collapse, throwing the victim down into a very smelly hole that could cause suffocation and death. Sometimes the covers aren't even visible, as they become covered with grass, dirt and weeks over the years. There was a case of that happening recently, when a child playing in a vacant lot crashed through the cover, into the cavity below. A couple of people jumped in to hold the child up so he could breathe, until ladders, ropes and other rescue equipment could be let down into the hole. What a trauma for kids and adults alike!

Deer, Deer, Deer!

The sellers' divorce has escalated from 'messy' to 'nasty'. The husband took three humongous deer antler chandeliers out before my buyer closed escrow. My buyer didn't want the antlers, but would have liked something other than wires hanging down.

Target Practice!

When I called to make an appointment, the listing realtor told me not to worry about the bullet holes in the house I was showing, as they would be fixed before closing. My buyers opted not to look in that neighborhood!

Rest In Peace

One house had a pet cemetery in the back yard. All the little graves were lined up with crosses--one wonders how so many pets all died there-- at least 15.

In The Pink!

One house had all pink plaster walls, and for texture, they had added straw. So there was straw everywhere, falling off the pink walls. You would have had to strip right down to the studs to get rid of it.

Thoughtful Seller

A lovely house, had all the latest gadgets, except the lever was missing from the high end Grohe kitchen faucet, and you had to turn on the faucet with the wrench that the seller had thoughtfully left for that purpose.

Rip Van Winkle Has Nothing On This One

I am the proud holder of the longest short sale in the valley-- nine months-- so far no one has been able to beat that one. If you want to bid on short sales, don't count on anything happening in a hurry. My buyers wanted that particular house in that particular neighborhood, so they were willing to wait that long. For the nine month wait, they went to 'their' new house often, did weeding, lawn mowing, tree trimming, and made friends with all their new neighbors. The neighbors kept a watch on the house for vandals or damage, and my people got invited to the block parties and were made welcome long before they moved in. The bank was certainly frustrating though.

Mold? Termites? What?

The house had parallel, vertical, black streaks on all the walls. Was it mold? A new kind of termites? When tested, the black streaks washed off, and turned out to be carbon from the candles the seller burned all the time. She was a dealer for candle parties and she frequently held parties at her home, and the carbon stuck to the walls wherever there were studs in the walls, for some reason.

Stairway to Nowhere..Anywhere, Please

This house had a lovely deck, overlooking the pool, but no door to get out there from the house, and no stairs to get up there from the yard-- just decorative I guess. Strange.

A Room Within A Room Without a View

In one bedroom of a house I was listing, there was a portable sauna, the same size as the room, which would be dismantled and taken out by the seller before closing. I suggested taking it out now, so buyers could see the room, and the seller was offended because she was so proud of her sauna. I said that not everyone was a sauna fan, plus we needed to make sure there were no problems or damage once it was removed. Since she was going to take it with her anyway, she finally agreed to take it out and store it until she moved into her new home.

Hazardous Waste Dump

An inspection revealed that a house in a multi-million dollar neighborhood, had housed a home business auto repair shop many years ago. All that was left was a hazardous waste oil pit where they had poured all the oil from oil changes for many years. I don't know how they managed to clean it up, but I'm glad my clients didn't buy it.

The Cows Were Here First

People forget that most residential lots at one time were farmland or desert, even those right in the middle of downtown. Out on a farm, there was no trash pickup, so trash had to be disposed of in whatever way was the easiest and cheapest method back then. Later, when residential lots were measured out, people had no idea what was underground. One appraiser tells the story that a buyer decided to add a few hundred square feet to his new home. In the course of digging to add footings, he discovered several rusted out stock tanks, buried standing on end, right where he wanted to build his new addition. Of course they had to be removed before construction could carry on.

What Size Is My Lot Again?

A hundred and fifty years ago, people usually didn't have surveys to tell them where to build. Lots were laid out wherever, and fences may or may not be right on the lot lines. In one upscale subdivision, once the city started doing surveys, it was found that the lots on several streets, actually extended eight feet into the alleys behind the lots. As well, the roads in front of those houses, also extended eight feet into the front of all the lots.

All these problems were grandfathered in, so no one was going to make the homeowners move their lots or the roads. However, one buyer could not be convinced that her lot was the correct size. She was adamant that she was losing those eight feet, so her taxes should be that much less. She couldn't see where the eight feet of what should have been roadway was in the front of her lot to make up for the eight feet in back that was in the alley.

Ancient Building Standards

Many years ago, builders didn't have cribbing standards. Cribbing is the process of using the forms that concrete contractors use to pour basements. Nowadays, you would pour footings, then add the plywood forms, and pour concrete into the forms, for a uniform thickness of basement walls. The footings plus the floor which is poured later, allow the walls to remain upright, plus bear the weight of the house being built.

One hundred years ago, to build a basement, you would dig a trench the size of the house footprint, and pour concrete into the dirt trench. Once it was dry, you would dig out the center of the trench, and dig out farther down, enough so that you could pack more concrete by hand onto the dirt under your original pour. You would continue this dig, then pack more concrete vertically onto the dirt, until you had the right height for your basement. Then without footings, you would pour the floor, and hopefully the house would be stable enough to stay upright for many years. Trouble was that the further down you dug, the narrower the concrete walls became, until the two foot wide walls that you started with at the ceiling of your basement, dwindled down to about six inches width at the bottom. You can see that a narrow, lighter weight amount of concrete at the bottom, was holding up a much wider and heavier weight at the top.

One such wall, in the process of being renovated, suddenly slid out from the dirt, taking most of the basement with it. When an engineer was engaged to give an opinion on the stability of the structure, he was tasked with telling the homeowner that the house was unstable, and would have to be completely demolished.

To add insult to injury, when the engineer went up into the attic to look at the structure, he found that the hundred year old house had hand hewn side beams that were attached to the center beam with ancient, extremely brittle leather straps. An expensive lesson before the days of home inspectors, who might not have found the concrete problem but most certainly would have found the leather strap problem!

Chapter 9 Horror Stories

Cat Attack! Cat Attack!

A realtor in Vancouver BC was showing a house where there was a feral cat with kittens in the house. It attacked her and her clients, scratching and biting, and all three of them were injured. Apparently the owner had rescued the cat, but hadn't told the realtor it was there. Lovely! And the realtor lost the sale too!

Cat Urine or Something Much Worse?

We walked in to a house that was basically a wreck. My buyer was a builder who had intended to buy it, fix it up and flip it. There were no carpets, and a strong cat urine smell, as well as bleach overloading the urine smell. There were also dark yellow stains on the walls and in all the sinks and on counters. Even the ground outside was discolored, as was the pool.

We have to take courses for real estate in hazards and disclosure of same, so I was pretty sure the house had been used as a meth house. My client agreed, and we left quickly, as prolonged exposure to the chemicals used to manufacture meth are harmful to anyone, but especially the very young and the elderly.

I called the listing realtor to tell her my suspicions, and she flatly refused to believe that the house could have been used for that purpose. Her reasoning? The seller lived next door, was elderly and was doing his best to clean up the smell with bleach. I asked if the house had ever been used as a rental, and she replied in the affirmative.

I suggested that perhaps the renters had been making meth there, and her seller wasn't aware of it. She refused to believe that either. Nor would she believe that her elderly seller could get sick from exposure and mixing bleach with the other chemicals in the house.

I did report it to the police, and they said they were aware of it as a meth house, but that since it was empty now, they couldn't do anything about it. I have to hope that whoever bought it bulldozed it, although even that doesn't take away the danger. If chemicals were spilled outside, it would affect plant growth, and could very well seep into groundwater, or affect the water supply to the house and pool.

Bugs Everywhere - How Not to Sell a House

Bugs, bugs everywhere–how not to sell a house in Arizona: Three brand new houses, same subdivision, full of crawling bugs. My buyers were completely turned off the whole area, and especially that particular builder.

My bug expert said they were either flying ants, or termites. In either case, we couldn't wait to get out. The funny part was when the listing agent called to get feedback on the houses, she WOULD NOT believe HER houses had bugs! She told me I must be mistaken, or that I didn't have the right address of HER listings. I suggested that if she checked her listings once a week, she might see the bugs herself.

More Bugs—Stay Calm!

In that same subdivision there were also two houses, which were being treated for Africanized or Killer Bees! Would you want to look at a house where the MLS listing said there were Killer Bees present? Neither would I or my buyers.

My bug expert says that 65% of bees they treat in Arizona nowadays are Africanized Killer Bee hybrids, as the original Killer bees have now mated with the regular bees.

The swarms love all the abandoned or bank owned houses, where they can live unmolested for months. They get inside the walls of houses, and you have to tear the drywall off, and sometimes the outside siding or stucco or the roof, to get at the hives & honeycombs.

Some banks just send in someone to smoke bomb the bees, which kills them, but leaves the hives/honeycombs intact. Other bees can smell the honey from up to 4 miles away, and new bees will just head on over and take over the hives/honeycombs left behind. To truly get rid of them you have to get rid of all traces of the hives.

If you ever see a bee swarm, try and get away quickly and quietly and call an exterminator. We see the swarms mostly in houses where no one lives, or has not lived for some time, and in one case a house we planned to look at had yellow caution tape around the yard, with signs stating 'Watch out for killer bees!' It's hard to get the bank that owns the houses to do anything that costs money, but then they never get the houses sold either!

Determined little critters

Months after I had sold them a house, my clients called to complain that there were termites in their coffee table in the living room! When the bug man got there to investigate, they had to pull up the carpet. There was a large crack in the slab, which couldn't have been seen by the inspector beforehand, but which went right through to the dirt beneath the slab. Those determined little critters had found a way to come up from the ground through the carpeting, and into the delicious coffee table. Not only did they have to have the termites treated, but had to repair the slab, and buy new carpeting.

Black Bumblebees?

If you see large black bumblebees flying around, here in Arizona, they are not bees, but a form of beetle. They don't bite, so no fear, but they do bore into exposed wood, to make nests. The best way to get rid of them is to call an exterminator, but painting the exposed wood with teak oil keeps them from coming back. However, they are pretty scary if you have never seen them before & they do make a loud noise.

London Bridge Is Falling Down

Great house, great neighborhood, great price. So what was the problem? The block retaining wall/fence behind the house, and about fifteen feet uphill from the house, belonging to a commercial building, was leaning precariously downhill toward the house. It had been water eroded, & cars from the parking lot above had run into the wall, which looked like it would fall into the yard & onto the house at any moment. The bank that owned it refused to do anything about it, like contact the commercial building manager or have an erosion test done, or shore up the fence, so my buyer walked. Banks get away with anything these days.

The Sopranos Must Have Lived Here!

I went to show a house built in 1994, which hadn't been

cleaned since it was new. That wasn't the worst part. The worst was that in one of the bedrooms, there was brown spatter all over the walls, fan, ceiling, floor, window, that looked suspiciously like blood spatter! E-w-w-w. Why doesn't the bank clean up stuff like that before it goes on the market? If there was a murder or suicide in the house, it's a disclosure issue, & people have to be told, so they can make up their minds if they want to live there or not. I know I wouldn't want to live there! However, if the house looks like a murder or suicide scene, even if it's just paint or ketchup, the chances of it getting sold are just that much less.

Maybe The Sopranos Lived Here Too!

A house not far from my own house, was the focus of police activity for several days. The media reported that a body had been found in the garage, packed in a trunk. It had been there for some time, but since it was winter, and everything was frozen, no one had noticed anything until spring. Once spring thaw occurred, blood started to seep out, and the smell was horrendous. It took a few weeks for the police to complete their investigation, and for the body to be removed and the garage cleaned up.

Then the house was put on the market for sale. Since the body wasn't found inside the house, it didn't need to be disclosed. The police also thought the person had been killed elsewhere and the body stashed in the garage later.

My buyers wanted to see the house but although it was not strictly a disclosure issue, I felt they had a right to know about the history of the garage. They decided not to buy it because of that. I always feel better disclosing stuff like that, because if I don't, I can be sure the neighbors will tell them after they move in!

More Soprano Stories

This week, there was a Florida news report that a client had contacted a hit man to 'off' his realtor. Fortunately for the realtor, the contact was an undercover police officer, so the client was arrested and the realtor spared. The client wasn't saying why he wanted his realtor dead, and the realtor doesn't know either. Best to keep on the good side of everyone!

Another one...

I heard this from an appraiser called to evaluate a home for estate purposes. A brother & sister were at odds over the estate & she tried to have the brother whacked. She paid a homeless person $10,000 cash and showed him where to put the body. The homeless guy went to the brother and told him, "Your sister really hates you!". He gave the money to the brother and left. The brother wants him for a witness to prosecute the sister but they can't find him now.

And Just One More...

I saw in the news, a new homeowner taking possession of his house in Florida, found a dead body in a car in the garage! Surprise! He likely thought the previous owners had left him the car as a bonus! Imagine not being able to move into your new house because of an ongoing police investigation!

Disclosure of Deaths, Murders etc.

There was a house in an upscale neighborhood where the husband shot the wife, and then himself. Regarding disclosure, we are not required to disclose such things after the first time the house sells after the event. That is, I have to tell you, the buyer, about the murder-suicide if you are the first buyer after the crime, but then once you buy it and decide to sell it later, you are not required to disclose its history.

As I said above, I prefer to disclose stuff like that, even though I am not required to do so, because certainly the neighbors will tell the buyers at any time in the future. In fact, some 30 years later, kids in that area won't go there at Hallowe'en, and they call it the Murder House or the Ghost Killer House. Would you want to have that moniker on your home?

Chapter 10 Snake Stories

We have a lot of snakes in Arizona. Actually there are lots of snakes in Canada too, but I never ran across strange snake stories till I started selling real estate in Arizona. I found I had enough to have a separate chapter about these critters. I certainly don't want to scare anyone away with snake and critter stories, because most residents will never see such pests in the course of daily living here.

I have never personally seen any kind of snake (except the ones I wrote about in this book, which have their own stories! There is a snake hotline that you can call if you ever happen to see one, and they will come and take it away. The chances of seeing snakes multiplies the farther out of the main areas of the city you go.

Snakes! Why Do There Have To Be Snakes?

A home inspector told me this one. When he went to open the electrical box, he found a dead mouse that had tried to escape a snake. However, the determined snake had managed to wriggle up into the box, and had been electrocuted. The inspector was faced with the choice of removing both dead bodies before he could test out the electrical in the house, or calling the power company.

He postponed his inspection until the power company could come out and remove the evidence and certify that the box was safe to inspect.

More Snakes

A brand new homeowner had a new dishwasher delivered, She and her husband opened up the carton, pulled out the shiny new appliance, and when they opened the door, found a guest in the form of a rattlesnake had taken up residence inside. They quickly closed the door, locked it and called the dealer to come and get it as quickly as possible. They hauled it outside, preferring not to have it in the house at all. No fear someone would steal it before the appliance people showed up, if they could hear the rattling tail inside!

Snake Stranger Danger!

The Phoenix TV news reported the other day that a listing realtor went over to an empty Scottsdale house to check on it. In the summer especially we have to check once a week for critters, flush the toilets, turn on the dishwasher, clothes washer, and all the faucets. This helps to keep the pipes from cracking with the heat, especially the plastic piping.

The realtor heard strange noises from the garage, and

when he opened up to investigate, found five– count 'em, five– diamondback rattle snakes had taken up residence in the garage! Scary!

Love Is a Many Splendored Thing

It was a tossup whether to put this story in the Naked chapter, the strange seller chapter, the pet chapter, or here, but it could be in any of those chapters.

A realtor arrived to show a house, after making an appointment with the sellers. There was no answer to the doorbell, so they used the lockbox and went in. She hollered 'Realtor' but there was no answer. The house tour went fine, and the client was interested in it, until they got to the master bedroom. There, in the bed, fast asleep, were the master and mistress of the house, naked, entwined in each other's arms, and totally surrounded by their pet boa constrictor, which was wound tightly around both of them!

The prospective buyer ran screaming from the house, followed quickly by the realtor.

Chapter 11 Realtor Versus Nature

Real! Dead! Nature!

The sellers were big game hunters and had hunted all over the world. They were also a taxidermist's best friend because they had stuffed and preserved all their best animals in all their glory. Not just the heads either. They had set up in every room of the house, dioramas including rocks, trees, hills, small mountains, and other natural elements, so that the stuffed animals looked more like they were in a zoo or the great outdoors, than a house. In fact they looked so realistic that I nearly jumped out of my skin when I came around the corner into the dining room and a fully erect seven foot grizzly bear nearly tapped me on the shoulder!

The next problem was that when you take three or four feet by the length of a room out of the room with a diorama, you make your rooms much smaller, so a buyer can't figure out if his king sized bed will fit in the room.

In another house, every room had stuffed pheasants and ducks seemingly flying out of every wall. Yet another had moose, deer, javelina, buffalo, elk, reindeer, mountain sheep and goats, (heads only here) mounted everywhere. In this day and age of conservationists, you never know who is going to be looking at your house while it's for sale, so just to ensure that you aren't excluding that element of buyer, it's better to get rid of the animals and repair the walls before listing. It's not just conservationists who dislike the stuffed animals, but most people find it creepy.

Bat Cave?

Workers in Florida taking off roof tiles to install a new roof, found thousands of bats living underneath the tiles. What would you feel like if that was your house or one you were considering buying? I'm sure the bat guano smell would have been pretty bad too.

Quail Attack!

Mary's funny real estate stories are not so funny when it's our house! A quail fell down our chimney and flew/pooped/hid everywhere all day before we could get him to leave.

Pepe LePew and All His Relatives?

I took a listing and then decided to do an open house. Nothing had been said up till this time, but sellers told me as they were leaving for the afternoon, not to disturb the skunk family under the front porch! Just what I needed to know prior to welcoming prospective buyers to the home!

Another Skunk Story

The seller told us that there was a window well surrounding the basement bedroom window, where a skunk liked to hang out. They had tried to get rid of it, but it had dug down under the window well, and kept returning, presumably to stay warm next to the house at night. It had sprayed the window screen, and the smell was starting to permeate the room. They said they were certain it was only a temporary situation, and that buyers should overlook the unwanted guest! Not very likely!

Scorpions, Oh My!

We have a lot of scorpions in Phoenix. They are quite territorial, and also quite resilient. Pest eliminators will try and tell you that if you spray and get rid of the bugs that scorpions like to eat, they will go away. Not so. Scorpions can survive for a couple of years underground with no food or water, and just when you think you've gotten rid of them, back out they come. Their bites can be painful, but are seldom serious unless you are allergic, elderly or very young. There are some things you can do to avoid them getting into the house, like spread diatomaceous earth around the slab, as well as the rest of the yard.

However, in one new home subdivision, a couple was mystified after they moved in, because they had lots of scorpions while their neighbors had none. I did some research with the Desert Botanical Garden, and was told that cats are impervious to scorpion stings, and actually like to play with scorpions, because they skitter around and the cats can chase them. Because cats also like to bring gifts to the people of the house, like mice or dead birds, they will also bring scorpions into the house. This couple had a couple of cats, and found the little biters in beds, shoes and other uncomfortable places in the house, until they made sure their cats stayed indoors. Suddenly the scorpion sightings stopped. Problem solved!

Elevated Sleep

I saw a house on tour that was raised off the floor several inches, by strange looking black plastic things. I asked another realtor about them and was told that hardware stores and pest people sell these if there are lots of scorpions around. They are shaped like an upside down cup, so that the bugs can't climb up into the bed. We concluded that there must be lots of them around to warrant the cups on every bed. Another clue was a black light on the nightstand, which is one of the ways you can see scorpions at night.

In one neighborhood, a couple of good old boys take their pellet guns out a couple of times a month, locate scorpions with black lights, and use them for target practice! I hope I never live in an area where that takes place.

What in the World is a Roof Rat?

Another pest that crops up every once in a while is the roof rat. They are small rats that like to get in to your attic to build nests, and eat electrical wiring. It's easy to keep them out, by ensuring there is no way to enter the attic from outside, utilizing screening over soffit air vents, and by taking away the rats' food source, which is citrus fruit. If you find your citrus has a hole in it, with the insides scooped out, and the outside skin is left hanging in the tree, it's a good bet there are roof rats in the neighborhood. Harvest all citrus early, and don't leave any fruit hanging around, and you should be good. The only time I ever saw an actual roof rat, was a dead one in our pool, plus our neighbors needed an exterminator to get rid of the ones that had managed to get into their attic.

Green Pools

With all the foreclosures, a few years ago, there were lots of neglected pools here. One was so green with algae and junk that you could hardly see the frogs swimming there. Kids with my buyers wanted to keep the green pool and frogs as pets!

In another pool someone had discarded an old mattress. Good Luck getting that waterlogged old thing out of there!

There was a nearly empty pool, lovely color of avocado green, with a pile of yucky waste carpet in the bottom growing lots of unidentifiable plants/creatures. Shivers!

Yet another buyer complained that her pool wasn't working. Her Home Inspector had said that the pool equipment was mostly missing and what was still there was in pieces. After closing buyer was upset green pool wasn't cleaning itself up. She thought cleaning was separate from the missing stuff.

Strange things we find in pools-- even our own—baby snakes, black widow, camel and brown recluse spiders, roof rats, mice, salamanders, geckos, baby rabbits and birds-- thank heaven they are all dead, & only found one at a time. Since we never see the pests outside, we think that birds drop them as they are flying past.

Does The Lister Really Think This One Should Be On The Market?

One house had (seemingly) dark tinted windows all around. There was no lockbox, so couldn't get in to see it. We later got in to find the entire interior was black with smoke and the whole inside had been burned.

Who's On First? Apparently you can fight City Hall or the FHA

I found this one on the internet & loved it enough to include here:

A New Orleans lawyer sought an FHA loan for a client. He was told the loan would be granted if he could prove satisfactory title to a parcel of property being offered as collateral. The title to the property dated back to 1803, which took the lawyer three months to track down. After sending the information to the FHA, he received the following reply.(Actual reply from FHA): "Upon review of your letter adjoining your client's loan application, we note that the request is supported by an Abstract of Title. While we compliment the able manner in which you have prepared and presented the application, we must point out that you have only cleared title to the proposed collateral property back to 1803. Before final approval can be accorded, it will be necessary to clear the title back to its origin." Annoyed, the lawyer responded as follows: (Actual response):"Your letter regarding title in Case No.xxxx has been received. I note that you wish to have title extended further than the 206 years covered by the present application. I was unaware that any educated person in this country, particularly those working in the property area, would not know that Louisiana was purchased by the United States from France, in 1803 the year of origin identified in our application. For the edification of uninformed FHA bureaucrats, the title to the land prior to U.S. ownership was obtained from France, which had acquired it by Right of Conquest from Spain. The land came into the possession of Spain by Right of Discovery made in the year 1492 by a sea captain named Christopher Columbus, who had been granted the privilege of seeking a new route to India by the Spanish monarch, Queen Isabella. The good Queen Isabella, being a pious woman and almost as careful about titles as the FHA, took the precaution of securing the blessing of the Pope before she sold her jewels to finance Columbus's expedition...Now the Pope, as I'm sure you may know, is the emissary of Jesus Christ, the Son of God, and God, it is commonly accepted, created this world. Therefore, I believe it is safe to presume that God also made that part of the world called Louisiana. God, therefore, would be the owner of origin and His origins date back to before the beginning of time, the world as we know it, and the FHA. I hope you find God's original claim to be satisfactory. Now, may we have our loan?" The loan was immediately approved.

I Think the Cat Owns This House

I took a listing, and while filling out paperwork in the kitchen, saw the family cat licking the JennAir grill which hadn't been cleaned in a long time. I had been a guest in that home for many dinners and parties, but vowed then and there, never to eat at this friend's house again. I gently recommended staging, and professional cleaning before marketing.

Alfred Hitchcock's "The Birds"

A realtor went to show a house, couldn't get in as the wrong code was on the MLS for the construction lockbox. When she called to ask how to get in, the listing realtor said he couldn't come over to let them in, because he didn't know where the house was! When she finally found someone who knew the lockbox code, she opened the door, and several grackles flew out, dive bombing her and her clients. Apparently they had gotten into the attic, built nests, and then descended into the house proper through the attic access which had been left open for some reason. (Grackles are annoying, noisy birds, somewhat like a magpie)

Jiminy Cricket!

It's cricket season here in Arizona in early to late spring and summer. Mostly crickets are harmless. They don't bite, birds like them for food, and a monthly spray of the house & yard keeps them down. But they do eat holes in clothing, just like moths. And if you've ever tried to get to sleep when one of them is 'singing' in your bedroom, they are very annoying!

Nice Kitty, Pretty Kitty...

I got this story from our pool man. He went out back

to clean the pool, and found that a family of bobcats had taken up residence. They can get nasty if disturbed or hungry, so he decided discretion is the better part of valor, and left quickly. I have no idea how the owner got rid of them.

Chapter 12 Realtor Versus Realtor

Rub-A-Dub-Dub

I heard this from another agent. A new agent from his firm did an open house; the sellers arrived home at 4pm expecting the agent to leave. He explained he couldn't leave yet because his clothes weren't dry-- that's right, he had brought his laundry to do at their house during open house. No word on whether the selle

Guess Who's Coming For Dinner?

I heard this one the other day and thought maybe the agent needed to re-think his occupation-- A homeowner had their agent do an open house, and came home to find he had eaten the entire Easter ham they were going to serve to their guests that evening. Amazing how people's minds work! Did he honestly think they wouldn't notice?

It's A Hard Knock Life

Not all these stories are mine personally, and this one certainly isn't. I was told by a seller that their previous realtor had been swimming naked in their pool with his girlfriend when the sellers arrived home. What a surprise for both couples! Lucky for me I was the second realtor they interviewed.

Some Realtors Should Never Think They Are Photographers!

Some MLS photos are good, some bad, but some are hilarious. One set of photos showed a master bedroom, with the owner still in bed! Couldn't the realtor wait a minute till the person got up & made the bed?

Another realtor obviously didn't realize that when you take a photo in a bathroom where there are mirrors, that you can be seen in the mirror when the photo is taken. There she was in all her glory, taking a photo of the bathroom, & she was topless! Maybe the a/c was turned off & she was hot taking all those photos?

Or Maybe Realtor Versus Home Inspector?

My husband, the home inspector, lost his superkey that allows us to open realtor lockboxes. He had to go get a new one. Two weeks later, I went to get keys to a house I had sold & the seller said she had found a superkey, asked me to turn it in. Guess who it belonged to?

Do You Hand Out Closing Gifts? Do You Deserve One?

This story is from a realtor, who gave 30% referral

fee to another realtor, 25% commission to her broker, accepted 1% less commission from bank, only to be confronted by her clients, who DEMANDED a closing gift. My opinion of closing gifts? Do you give a gift to the grocer/plumber for good service? Realtors do a bangup job under trying circumstances, for less money, more headaches, so maybe realtors deserve a gratuity for good service!

You Can Fool Some Of The People Some Of The Time

The buyer told us during the inspection that he would be replacing the picture window in the living room with sliding glass doors. Then his realtor presented my seller with a request for repairs for $500 because the picture window had lost its thermal seal! My seller refused because the buyer had told us about his plan to replace it. The buyer's realtor told me he thought it was worth a try because my elderly sellers might just pay for it, if they didn't know better. That's why they had a good realtor!

When First We Practice To Deceive

This is from a realtor with 30+ years of experience. She says this is the first time she has been truly speechless in all that time. She had a referral from an old client that a lady wanted to sell her rental condo. The realtor picked up the owner & they went to look at the condo, which was supposed to be vacant. When they opened the door, they heard noises, & found the lady's husband naked with his secretary! The realtor & the lady backed out of the door, as the husband was saying the classic words, "But Honey, it's not what you think, I can explain…". The realtor didn't get the listing, because now the husband is living in the condo as part of the divorce settlement!

You Can Try And Fool People, But Better Not To

A nervy builder charged a lot premium for a house that supposedly backed onto a wash. The only trouble was that the 'wash' was actually a utility right of way with power poles in it! Some premium lot! Most people don't want to back up to power poles because of the high voltage, danger & even the belief that living next to the lines affects fertility!

Do You Want To Sell This House Or Don't You?

I couldn't get hold of listing realtor to get a mechanical lockbox code after many tries. The buyers & I were about to leave when we took a look at the backyard, & found the patio door wide open. And they wonder why houses get vandalized.

How Many Bathrooms in This House?

The MLS said the house had 3 bedrooms, 2 baths. We discovered that one bathroom was in the master suite. The other, which had been the hall bath, had been walled off the hall, & a door cut through from a secondary bedroom to what used to be the hall bath. The owner told us he wanted his teenage daughter to have her own bathroom. However, what about guests wanting to use the bathroom? Or the pre-teen son, who had to go through the teenage princess' bedroom to get to the bathroom? Some people have strange ideas of what is or is not acceptable in a house. I'm not sure what I would have said if it had been my listing, but my buyers were not impressed with the set up.

What's Included In The Sale?

Years ago, before landscaping was included in the items for sale in the contract, one couple who had loved the streetscape and curb appeal of their new house, arrived with their moving van to discover that the previous owners had removed every flower, every pot, every tree and bush, every foot of sod, even the largest trees that would have required a tree mover.

We have all heard stories about lovely new appliances which were removed by the sellers and replaced with second hand, mismatched appliances. That's why we take photos of everything so we know what's there. One seller's realtor saved the day for the buyers, because his pictures in the MLS clearly showed the high end stainless steel appliances, not the harvest gold and avocado green ones that were left by his sellers.

One sale nearly cratered for me when the seller wanted to take her antique butcher block with her. It wasn't attached, and hadn't been requested in the contract by the buyer, but nevertheless the buyer wanted it. Both parties were threatening to cancel the sale because of the butcher block. I even went to several antique stores to find one, with no luck. I finally convinced my seller, that it wouldn't fit in her new house anyway, so she left it.

Another sale hinged on if the seller was going to leave an upside down wrought iron black fish skeleton whose ribs were used in the bathroom to hold fingertip towels. The seller had received it as a gift, and wanted to keep it. The buyer wouldn't budge and said she would cancel the deal if she didn't get it. Again, I went looking for something similar that would keep both people happy, again with no luck. Finally the beleaguered seller decided to leave it behind, rather than lose the sale.

Chapter 13 Stories That Don't Fit Anywhere Else But Should Be Included

No Forwarding Address

Years ago, my cousin was staying part time for the summer at our Granddad's. He was out on the road working, came back, walked in to see a strange lady in a bathrobe, with curlers in her hair. They introduced themselves & the lady said she had bought the house the week before. Grampa hadn't bothered to tell my cousin the house was sold!

I Love My Clients

I was showing a house where the seller's young daughter needed brain surgery. Her father asked me to hand out fund raiser cards at my office. My client pulled out a $100 bill & contributed on the spot. I love my clients.

Art Is In The Eye Of The Beholder

One seller was a prolific artist. She was so prolific, she had canvasses stacked 10 deep on every wall in the house, along with floor to ceiling art completely covering every wall, even in the bathrooms, kitchen, (Including the kitchen cupboard doors!), laundry, garage, and on every door in the house. They were on easels, tables, even the top of the washing machine. I don't think she gave any away, or sold any.

One Person's Art is Not another Person's Art

One client had a three foot by five foot painting in the living room that showed a hand, holding a large knife, about to slash into a watermelon, except the that knife was dripping copious amounts of blood. I thought perhaps it was a bit graphic for potential buyers who might be turned off. My seller loved the painting and told me it cost thousands of dollars. I was finally able to get her to take it down and store it till after the sale.

An Interior Decorating Lesson Or a Child Behavior Lesson?

A father who was upset that his kids constantly tracked in dirt, had all the carpets taken up and black linoleum installed– even in the kitchen, baths and bedrooms. Unfortunately, no one told him that mud shows up just as badly on black as on lighter colors.

Gift With Purchase

During the real estate 'bust' around 2005 to 2007, many

people here were so anxious to sell their houses that they were offering vintage Mustangs, Hummers, Cadillacs, Corvettes in the garage to go along with the house at no extra cost.

Bring A Flashlight

I had made sure my client could get keys at midnight when he arrived from the airport to take possession of his new home. He couldn't see in the dark to turn the power on, so he slept without heat or light till the power company told him how to turn on breakers the next day. & yes, we do need furnaces in AZ sometimes.

Free Fruit In Every Yard

We have lots of citrus fruit on the trees here now. My clients from Canada think it's great that you can just pick it off the trees & eat it while we are out looking at houses! It's also great to have fresh squeezed orange juice and grapefruit for breakfast every day at home. You can't do that back in Canada– the best you can do there is crabapples in summer, & the occasional saskatoons.

Good Karma

Gotta love the karma of showing houses. I was showing new model homes one day to a couple from Calgary,

& another couple from Calgary was touring the same house! We have known each other for many years, but they didn't know my husband & I lived here full time now. Then I had two clients instead of one!

Good Neighbor? Welcome Wagon? Or What?

I sold a building lot to a family, who proceeded to build their dream house. There were three more houses being built at the same time on the same street. The owners and the builders kept finding small gifts, trinkets, coins, broken toys, and articles of clothing both inside and outside the houses. Construction workers often found a woman sleeping in the houses when they came to work, and sometimes she had a man with her. When they tried to roust her out, she claimed that she lived there, and showed them her clothing and bedding to prove it.

Sometimes she would sit on the balconies or decks, naked or nearly naked, but she didn't seem violent, just delusional, claiming all the incomplete houses were hers. The workers and owners often threw out bags of garbage and used clothing left by her, and she left her mark often, once windows were installed, as she left red lipstick 'kisses' on all the glass.

Police were repeatedly called, and she was warned off. Finally the owners got a restraining order, but that didn't stop the woman either. The police told the owners that the woman was mentally ill and off her medications, but they didn't want to arrest her. They delivered her to her mother, who wasn't able to keep track of her all the time. And still the money, jewelry and toys continued to be left at all the doors, and hanging from trees and fences.

This continued until all the houses were completely closed in, and she wasn't able to get inside anymore. Then suddenly the gifts, kisses, and sleepovers stopped, and haven't recurred after a couple of years of occupancy. Unnerving to say the least.

Out of the Mouths of Babes

Buyers and I were at the escrow office to sign their deal. They had a three year old with them, who was quietly coloring while we waited for the escrow officer to join us.

Just as she walked through the door, the three year old passed gas, long and loudly. Innocently she looked up at her parents who were looking any direction except at her, and she said, quite calmly "Someone in here farted!" as she looked at the escrow officer. And then she went back to her coloring. When we had all smothered our laughter, her father asked, "Who do you think it was that farted?" She looked around at everyone in the room, and said "I guess it was me. 'Scuse me!"

Block Party Coming Up

Sold houses a block apart to two couples from Canada, who didn't know each other. I introduced them & now they are planning a block party for all the Canucks. Only rule: Mrs. Costco isn't allowed to be the caterer. Have to bring home made!

Manana! They Thought They Had Lots Of Time

When my buyer and I arrived to pick up keys after closing, we found the seller not yet moved out. My buyer had to cancel painters, locksmith, cleaners etc for two days till seller got all the stuff out.

Cool In Summer, Warm In Winter

One house I viewed was made of straw bales, with plaster over the straw on the inside, and stucco on the outside. The walls were about two feet thick. This construction type has great insulation value, and the sellers told us they didn't even need a/c, just fans. You'd think it might be a fire hazard, but the straw is so tightly packed, it won't burn.

The Perfect House

Why is it when some buyers find the perfect house, perfect area, perfect price, perfect everything, they still want to see a couple more houses, 'just to make sure'? And this after seeing about 25 houses?

Little Girl Lost

I was showing houses to parents of a delightful as well as well-behaved two year old girl who managed to get 'lost' in the vacant house. She was so quiet, hiding in a kitchen cupboard, we had a hard time finding her

Casey Jones

Would you buy a house that had a railway caboose sitting in the front yard? The seller used it for a guest house, and play house for grandkids, as he used to be a Railroad man.

Funny thing was, when the house finally sold, the lender insisted that we take a photo showing that the caboose had actually been removed from the property. The new owners were kind of sad, as they had hoped to have a free guest house. They found out later that the neighbors were glad it was gone.

I Love Past Client Referrals

Twelve years ago, I sold a house in Calgary. Their son, last year wanted to sell his house in Calgary. He googled me to sell it, found I now live in Phoenix, & now that the Calgary house is sold, he's buying a house in Phoenix from me! Gotta love old connections. Twelve years! Two different cities! Imagine!

Hire That Woman For Sales

I heard this one from our termite guy. One customer of his said she could get him the whole neighborhood for customers, so he said he'd give her a free year of termite treatment for every new customer she got him. She's up to twenty-three years of free treatments already!

Pray For the House To Sell

We walked into large white two storey foyer, complete with huge white-draped altar, religious statues, icons, burning candles, and several urns of ashes of dead relatives. Creepy!

They Bite!

A small child accompanying my buyers accidentally backed into a cactus—so we ended our house tour at emergency room. The boy tearfully told the doctor- you have to "watch those bushes 'cause they bite!"

Call The Plumber

My client heeded the call of nature, then flushed the toilet in an empty house, only to have it overflow, and we were left cleaning up as water flowed down the halls toward the carpet, with no towels, no toilet paper, nothing! Fun! Finally I was able to contact the seller's realtor who arrived with lots of towels. Boy, was my client's face red!

Be Prepared

Always make sure your car is full of gas before you take clients out to look at houses. One realtor told me she didn't do that, and ran out of gas about a mile from her office. She had to get another realtor to come and rescue her and her clients in 100 degree heat.

Kids Say the Darnedest Things

My clients and I were at the escrow office to sign closing

documents, and their very well behaved three year old girl was sitting at the end of the table, coloring. As the escrow officer came in, loaded down with documents, the little girl piped up, "Dad, it smells bad in here like somebody farted."

Her dad stared at her, while the rest of us were speechless with embarrassment. He asked, "Would that somebody be you?" and she answered, without looking up from her coloring, "Yeah, excuse me."

Lost and Found

A fellow realtor from my office told this story that happened several years ago. Her boyfriend's house was broken into while he was away, & the thieves had backed a moving truck up to the garage, & stolen everything in the house, including appliances, linens, dishes, electronics, even his clothes! A large number of bronze sculptures and other artwork were also taken. The police report was filed & with no sign of any of the stuff, insurance was collected.

Four years after the theft, this realtor was out showing houses, and walked into a house with her clients. She noticed that a lot of the furnishings and art in the house looked a lot like the items that had been stolen from her boyfriend, so she called him & he came and confirmed that the entire house was furnished with his stuff!

The seller of the house came home & said she had bought all the stuff at a garage sale four years ago, & when police were called, they refused to charge her with theft or even possession of stolen property.

The man asked if he could buy back the artwork and sculptures, and paid the seller a fraction of what they were originally worth, but the rest of his stuff was charged up as a loss, as even the insurance company didn't want to deal with the hassle of trying to prove who owned what, when, where and how.

Imagine the astronomical chances of that particular realtor walking into that particular house and recognizing all the stolen items! Amazing!

Realtor Heal Thyself

I was visiting a house to pick up keys, and managed to trip over the front step, which also had a gate I was hanging onto, and I dislocated my shoulder. Most painful thing I ever did, and took hours to get it fixed at the hospital. That ended my house showing plans for that day.

Be sure to pick up books by Mary Maxie too! Available from www.marymaxieauthor.com or www.amazon.com

Extraordinary Stories for Contemporary, Eclectic, Discriminating Readers!

Sophie's Calgary Stampede

A Washington corporate lawyer arrives in Calgary Alberta just in time for the annual ten days of madness called the Calgary Stampede. Feeling like a brown shoe with a tuxedo or a Manolo high heel with a cowgirl outfit, Sophie is about to find out what the new wild west is all about, as she is roped and kidnapped by Rowley, a real cowboy who takes her on an insider's trip around the Calgary Stampede. The parties, the lifestyle of the cowboy, and the love of a good man are all in her future, if she can do her job and show him what Washington really wants. Maybe she'll find out that what Washington wants and what Sophie wants are pretty close to the same thing.

Waiting for 9/11

A memorial to the women who waited on the fateful day of the attck on the World Trade Center, as well as to those who died there. Twenty-six stories of bravery, wonder, thanksgiving, and good or bad timing.

Teacher of Time- Theriesenstadt Concentration Camp

Two teachers travel back in time from the present to a concentration camp in Nazi Germany in 1943. Can they use modern communication techniques to contact the Allies and perhaps shorten the war? Can they rescue the unfortunate souls imprisoned in the camp?

Teacher of Time – Berlin Wall

Book Two of the Teacher Series. Another trip back in time from the present to 1961 Germany when the Berlin Wall was erected. Can our young hero manage to rescue a brilliant violinist from her dreary and endless existence behind the Wall?

Waiting For The Crest

2013 saw the once-in-a-lifetime flood of epic proportions in Calgary, Alberta Canada. The flooding occurred with a 'perfect storm' of events, which saw spring run off from the Rocky Mountains west of the city, coincide with heavy rains. The city is bisected by two large rivers, the Bow and the Elbow, and one or both rivers also run through Banff, Canmore, Bragg Creek, Cochrane and Exshaw. High River was flooded by the Sheep River. The crest of a flood is the high water mark, and once the crest is reached, flood water begins to recede.

The twenty-six stories here are representational and fictional, but are meant to show the emotions, frustrations, depression suffering, bravery, and thoughts of a variety of people affected by the widespread devastation.

Coming Soon by Mary:

Teacher of Time- Cambodia

A sequel to the first two Teacher Of Time novels, this one tells the story of the Cambodian Civil War, which is often overlooked in the shadow of the Viet Nam war. Our intrepid time travelers once again utilize the portal in the Phoenix Musical Instrument Museum to help fellow musicians in a land that was devastated by educational cleansing, and is now on its way back into the twenty-first century with help from a Phoenix couple who fund a school in Cambodia.

www.marymaxieauthor.com

mary@marymaxie.com

Follow Mary on Facebook and Goodreads

You might also enjoy these books by Patrizia Murray:

Marda's Muse

Feeling like Joan Wilder in Romancing the Stone, Marda is sniffling her way through allergy season, nearly finished her newest romance novel. Marda is the best friend of Justine, of Justine's Auction fame. Since Justine's marriage to Ryan, Marda has been feeling like a fifth wheel whenever she's around her friends. Now, as she finds herself wishing for a hero like those she writes about, opportunity for a new life is about to knock on her door. As she embarks on a Joan Wilder type adventure, will her life imitate her art? Logan is a most unlikely muse for Marda, but he turns out to be the best, the only, the sexiest muse ever! Now if only Marda can save several lives, including her own and Logan's, things will be great, won't they?

Lucinda's Grooms & Evalina's Gamble

These are the first and second in the Montgomery/Marquette saga, Although Evalina's Gamble stands alone, many of the same characters and locations begin in Lucinda's Grooms.

In 1914, Lucinda is loved by two cousins, Jack and Ford. She loves them both, but marries Jack. Ford comes home from the Great War in Europe with a small daughter, and professes his love for Lucinda once again. He proposes a scandalous solution that would allow the three of them to be together.

When they meet the family of Ford's first wife who was killed in France, they forge an economic alliance with the coal barons, to develop coal mining in their small Canadian town.

Can their three way love brave the town gossips and keep the Marquettes from taking their granddaughter away from them?

From rural Canada to Paris, the sweeping saga of the Montgomery family where love transcends all, and families are not what they seem.

Mia's Blind Date

While Rob is being held hostage by rebel forces who have kidnapped him from his oil rig job, Mia is about to marry Colby. After a hilarious meeting at a blind date, Mia and Rob have parted over his decision to leave her for two years and work in the volatile Mid-East. Rob dreams of returning to Mia, and Mia realizes she can't marry Colby till she finds out Rob's fate. Will she wait for Mr. Right or settle for Mr. Right Now?

Suzien's Second Love

Suzien has a settled but dull life with her son and both sets of her son's grandparents. She hasn't dated since her one true love was killed in a plane crash while she was pregnant. Can John, a man eleven years her junior, make her see that love knows no age? That he loves her for everything about her, not just her looks that may fade long before his looks do? Can the hot sex between them change Suzien's mind about being seen by the town and the grandparents as a cougar?

Freddi's Collection

Why do three separate buyers want the acreage that Freddi has inherited from her inventor father? What is the mysterious concrete structure on the property with no doors or windows? Is bad boy biker Brian on her side or the other side in the attempts to buy her out? Brian's motorcycle injuries give both of them time to think about what they really want from life, and to decide if their love can overcome the barriers they have set up against each other, and to solve the mysteries her father has left behind.

Hanna's Hat Trick, first in the Olympic Series

What happens when a self-confessed workaholic, Hanna Bowness, owns and manages a professional hockey team and is responsible for keeping the team's 'goon' or 'enforcer' under control? Rejean Haultain is big, bad, and beautiful, and up to now, totally untamed. It's up to Hanna to keep her team in the black, keep Rejean from beating opposition players black and blue, or hurting others to the point that her team is penalized, keep her heart from bleeding red, and to keep Rejean from serious injury or even jail. As the two skate around their desires and their jobs, as well as keeping the media out of their personal lives, and navigating the courts of public opinion in the midst of Olympic playoffs, and the Stanley Cup, is it even possible for the twain to meet? Or will Rejean's hat tricks be relegated to the ice, and not to Hanna's bedroom?

Justine's Auction

Rob and Justine are brought together for a Bachelor/Bachelorette auction in aid of Breast Cancer Research. Is the love they feel strong enough to transcend the health problems of Rob's sister Leah, and for Rob to learn to love in spite of his fears that Justine may fall prey to the disease too? In this book we meet Marda or Muarda's Muse for the first time. Justine also appears briefly in Marda's story.

Coming Soon by Patrizia Murray

Bella's Song

A melty chocolate voice that spans nearly four octaves, introduces Daniel to Bella, a soon-to-be-world famous singer of everything from opera to Broadway, with stops in between for a little jazz, a little country, and a little Rock 'n' Roll. He would follow that siren's call anywhere she led, but the threads that hold them together are mysterious and full of longing. He needs to make sure his songbird is safe from all that threatens her, including himself.

Author Bio:

Mary Maxie has been a newspaper reporter, columnist, editor and publisher. She has also been a librarian, social worker, human resources expert, and the owner of weekly newspapers plus a web printing plant that prints newspapers. She currently lives in Arizona, where she works as a realtor. She has been married to the same man for over 40 years, has one son, one daughter-in-law, and the three most gorgeous, gifted granddaughters in the world, the oldest of whom acts as beta reader & consultant.

See more of Mary on Facebook, where she responds to all friend requests. Check out book trailers and new publications on www.marymaxieauthor.com.

Made in the USA
Charleston, SC
19 December 2014